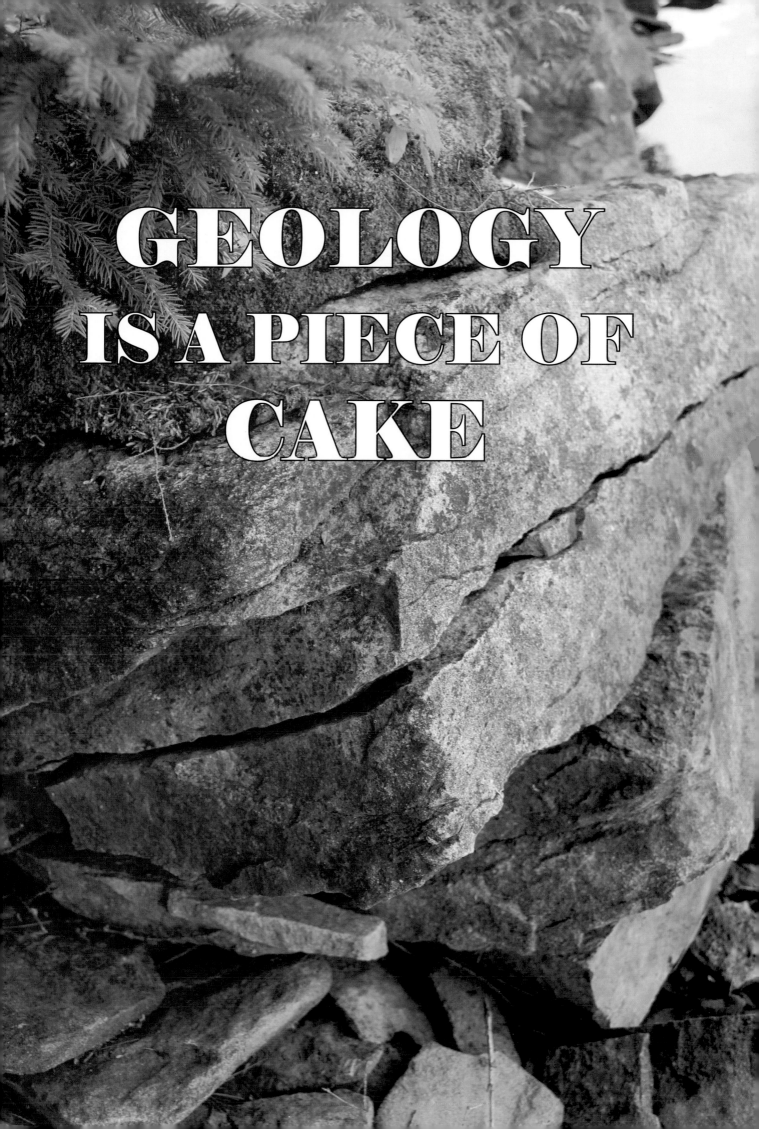

GEOLOGY IS A PIECE OF CAKE

For further information, contact:
Tumblehome Learning, Inc.
201 Newbury St, Suite 201
Boston, MA 02116
http://www.tumblehomelearning.com

Library of Congress Control Number: 2017930701
ISBN 978-1-943431-28-1

Coppens, Katie
Geology is a Piece of Cake / Katie Coppens - 1st ed

Design: Yu-Yi Ling

Printed in Taiwan
10 9 8 7 6 5 4 3 2 1

GEOLOGY
IS A PIECE OF CAKE

CAKE

KATIE COPPENS

DEDICATION

This book is dedicated to my students.

CONTENTS

WHAT IS GEOLOGY ?

Geology is the study of Earth. This includes learning about rocks, *minerals*, tectonic plates, fossils, and much more.

HOW DOES THIS RELATE TO CAKE ?

Throughout this book, cake will serve as a model to help you understand various concepts in geology.

ROCKS AND MINERALS

WHAT IS A ROCK ?

A rock is a nonliving substance that is made of minerals that have been compacted or melted together.

A variety of rock types

HOW DOES THIS RELATE TO CAKE ?

Picture a delicious, warm piece of carrot cake and all the ingredients used to make it, such as carrots, raisins, and cinnamon. The carrot cake itself is like a piece of rock and all the ingredients that come together to make it are like minerals.

Carrot cake and some of its ingredients

WHAT IS A MINERAL ?

While a rock is formed through different minerals compressing or melting together, a mineral is pure all the way through. A mineral is a nonliving substance that is made of a crystalline structure with a specific chemical composition. Some common minerals are quartz, feldspar, and muscovite. It doesn't matter if you have a small piece of quartz or a large piece of quartz, it still has the same chemical composition all the way through. However, when the minerals quartz, feldspar, and muscovite melt together, they slowly cool and harden to form the rock granite. If there was a recipe for how Earth makes granite it would look something like this:

GRANITE

⬦⬦⬦⬦⬦⬦⬦⬦⬦⬦⬦⬦⬦⬦

⅔ cup feldspar   ¼ cup quartz   1 pinch of amphibole

1 teaspoon of mica (either muscovite or biotite or a mixture of both)

1. Mix all ingredients.

2. Heat and melt all ingredients to 900 degrees Celsius deep in Earth.

3. Let cool slowly underground. Be aware, cooling can take <u>around a million years.</u>

Rose quartz and muscovite
(muscovite is a form of mica)

HOW DOES THIS RELATE TO CAKE ?

Carrots of various sizes
are the same composition
all the way through

Cinnamon, raisins, and carrots are like minerals because they are the same all the way through. If you take a nibble or a big bite of a carrot, it will have the same taste and the same chemical composition. By contrast, carrot cake is like a rock because the minerals form together to make it. If you take a bite of carrot cake, you will taste lots of different "minerals."

DOES A ROCK ALWAYS HAVE THE SAME MINERALS ?

Each kind of rock contains a specific combination of minerals. For example, basalt, which is an *igneous rock*, is primarily made of pyroxene, plagioclase, and olivine.

HOW DOES THIS RELATE TO CAKE ?

The ingredients to make a cake are like a recipe. You will find common ingredients in many cakes, such as flour and sugar, and the same is true for rocks. Because feldspar and quartz are the two most common rock-forming minerals on Earth, they are found in many types of rocks, just as flour and sugar are found in most types of cake.

"IGNEOUS ROCK" CARROT CAKE

2 cups all-purpose flour

1 teaspoon baking soda

1 teaspoon vanilla

2 teaspoons ground cinnamon

3 cups of shredded or "matchstick" carrots

1 cup canola or vegetable oil

1 ½ cups sugar

3 eggs

1 cup raisins

1 pinch of salt

1. Preheat oven to 350 degrees Fahrenheit. *The oven will represent the inside of Earth where intrusive igneous rocks form.*

2. Mix wet ingredients (eggs, oil, and vanilla) in a bowl. Next, stir in granulated sugar until it is blended in. Add other dry ingredients, with the final ingredients added being the carrots and raisins.

3. Apply cooking spray to the base and sides of a 9x13" pan. Dust with flour.

4. Add batter and make level. *The batter is like the magma that will slowly harden to become an intrusive igneous rock (to truly be like magma, the batter would be melted).*

5. Bake 40 minutes. *This cake serves as an intrusive igneous rock, which forms inside of the earth.* To make sure the cake is done, stick a toothpick in the center of the cake and remove it; the toothpick should come out dry.

6. Let cool completely before cutting and serving. *Intrusive igneous rocks cool slowly, which is why the crystals are easier to see than in extrusive igneous rocks.*

7. *While eating, pay attention to what "minerals" you can see that make up the igneous rock cake.*

ROCK TYPES

HOW MANY ROCK TYPES ARE THERE ?

All rocks fall under three categories: igneous rocks, *sedimentary rocks*, or *metamorphic rocks*.

WHAT IS AN IGNEOUS ROCK ?

An igneous rock is a rock formed from cooling *lava* or *magma*. Magma is melted, liquid rock below Earth's surface. When magma erupts from a volcano it is called lava. There are two types of igneous rocks, depending on where the liquid rock cools. If it cools and hardens below Earth's surface, it's an *intrusive* form of igneous rock. Some well known intrusive igneous rocks are granite, gabbro, and diorite. If the rock cools on the surface, it's *extrusive*. Some well known extrusive igneous rocks are basalt, obsidian, and pumice.

Lava from a volcano

HOW DOES THIS RELATE TO CAKE ?

A molten lava cake shows how an extrusive igneous rock forms. When the warm chocolate comes out of the molten lava cake, it will eventually cool and harden, much like the lava from a volcano.

Molten lava cake

WHAT IS A SEDIMENTARY ROCK ?

Asedimentary rock forms by small pieces of rocks or minerals being compressed together over a long period of time. Some well-known sedimentary rocks are sandstone, limestone, and shale. Often sedimentary rocks form near or under calm water. The calm water allows sediment to deposit and build up over time. The sediment then compacts together, and if buried below the water table, it goes through a process called cementation.

Other sedimentary deposits form on dry land, like gravel piled up at the foot of a mountain cliff. After gravel sediments get compacted and cemented, they turn into the rock called **conglomerate**.

Limestone, shale, and sandstone are examples of sedimentary rock

HOW DOES THIS RELATE TO CAKE ?

Coffee cake

Acoffee cake is much like a sedimentary rock. You can see crumbles throughout the cake, which are compressed much like the sediment grains in a sedimentary rock.

WHAT IS A METAMORPHIC ROCK ?

A metamorphic rock is a rock that experienced extreme pressure and some heat and changed into a new type of rock. The pressure for rock metamorphism normally comes from the tremendous squeezing of Earth's crust that produces mountain ranges. For example, limestone is a sedimentary rock, but if squeezed to become part of a mountain range, it can change into marble, which is a metamorphic rock. Limestone is often called the parent rock of marble. There are two categories of metamorphic rock: *foliated* and *non-foliated*. If a metamorphic rock forms with layers (or bands) it is called a foliated metamorphic rock. An example of a foliated metamorphic rock is gneiss. Quartzite is an example of a non-foliated metamorphic rock because it does not have layers.

Foliated gneiss

Non-foliated quartzite

HOW DOES THIS RELATE TO CAKE ?

A chocolate and vanilla layer cake can serve as an example of a foliated metamorphic rock because of the visible bands (layers). The confetti cake is an example of a non-foliated metamorphic rock.

Layered cake

Confetti cake

EXTRUSIVE MOLTEN LAVA CAKE

½ stick butter (at room temperature, plus some extra butter for ramekins)

½ cup of chocolate chips or chunks   ½ cup of powdered sugar

1 egg   1 egg yolk

3 tablespoons of flour

1. Preheat oven to 400 degrees Fahrenheit. *The oven will represent a volcano.*

2. Rub butter on the inside of two ramekins (base and sides).

3. Melt ½ stick of butter and the chocolate in a microwave-safe bowl for 30 seconds, then stir. Microwave for another 30 seconds and continue to stir until melted.

4. Stir the powdered sugar into the mix, then add the yolk and whites of one egg, then add just the yolk of another egg and stir. Add the flour to the mixture and stir until smooth. *This represents the magma of what will become an extrusive igneous rock.*

5. Divide the magma (cake batter) between the two ramekins. Do not fill magma all the way to the top.

6. Put ramekins on a cookie sheet and bake for 13-14 minutes.

7. Carefully remove the cookie sheet from the oven and let ramekins sit for one minute. Carefully take a butter knife and run it along the inside edge of the ramekins. This will help loosen the cakes.

8. With adult help (and oven mitts), flip the ramekin upside down over a plate. Carefully pull up the ramekin to release the cake.

9. *Cut into the middle of the cake to reveal the cake's chocolate lava. While eating, pay attention to the lava and how it can harden to represent an extrusive igneous rock.*

THE ROCK CYCLE

HOW LONG DOES IT TAKE A ROCK TO FORM ?

It depends on what type of rock it is and where it forms. A sedimentary rock could take thousands of years for the sediments to build up and compress, whereas some forms of igneous rock can cool and harden in days.

WHAT IS THE ROCK CYCLE ?

The **rock cycle** is the continual process of rocks changing form. Igneous rocks form when magma from Earth's mantle and lower crust cools and solidifies. Sedimentary rocks form when small pieces of mineral and rock are compressed and cemented together. With heat and pressure, both igneous and sedimentary rocks can re-bake into metamorphic rock. All three rocks types can also break down into smaller pieces of **sediment** and then, with time and pressure, become a sedimentary rock. All three rock types can be pushed down deep into the earth where they can melt into magma or re-bake into a new type of metamorphic rock, creating an endless cycle of possible reformation.

Sedimentary rock

Erosion, deposition and cementation

Melting and cooling

Changing temperature and pressure

Erosion, deposition and cementation

Melting and cooling

Metamorphic rock

Changing temperature and pressure

Igneous rock

Visual representation of the rock cycle

HOW DOES THIS RELATE TO CAKE ?

Cake can't change form like rocks, but let's pretend it can. A cake could have crumbs break off and compress together (sedimentary rock), re-bake into a new cake (metamorphic rock) or melt back into batter and harden into another type of cake (igneous rock).

Cake batter

ROCK AND MINERAL HARDNESS

DO ALL ROCKS HAVE THE SAME HARDNESS ?

Rocks are made of different minerals. Minerals have various levels of hardness, so therefore rocks have different levels of hardness.

HOW IS MINERAL HARDNESS MEASURED ?

The *Mohs scale* measures mineral hardness. On this scale, diamonds are the hardest, which is a 10. Talc is the lowest, which is a 1. Some other common minerals are apatite, which is a 5, and quartz, which is a 7. Mineral hardness is based on what can and cannot scratch it. For example, a piece of glass is a 5.5 on the Mohs scale, so it can scratch minerals like talc and apatite, but not minerals like quartz or diamond. A harder material can scratch a softer material, but a softer material cannot scratch a harder material.

Mohs Hardness Scale	Mineral Example	Observations
1	Talc	Fingernail will scratch it (very easily)
2	Gypsum	Fingernail will scratch it
3	Calcite	Knife will scratch it (very easily)
4	Fluorite	Knife will scratch it
5	Apatite	Knife will scratch it (with difficulty)
6	Feldspar	It will scratch glass (with difficulty)
7	Quartz	It will scratch glass (easily)
8	Topaz	It will scratch glass (very easily)
9	Corundum	It cuts glass
10	Diamond	It cuts glass (very easily)

HOW DOES THIS RELATE TO CAKE ?

If there was a Mohs scale for cake hardness, angel food cake would be one of the lowest and fruitcake would be one of the highest.

Angel food cake and fruitcake

HOW DOES MINERAL HARDNESS IMPACT ROCKS ?

Imagine a rock that is very hard, like granite, and a rock that is not as hard, like shale. If those two rocks were both exposed to pounding waves, shale would break down more easily and turn into sediment faster.

HOW DOES THIS RELATE TO CAKE ?

A cake could be classified on a scale by how easily it is cut by a knife. Angel food cake would fall lower on the scale than a layer cake, which would fall lower than a fruitcake. The higher the number a cake has on the scale, the more difficult it is to cut, chew, and break down into smaller pieces.

A knife cutting into a cake

WEATHERING AND EROSION

WHAT IS WEATHERING ?

Weathering is the process of rocks or minerals breaking down. Weathering that causes a physical breakdown or fragmentation of rock is called *physical* or *mechanical weathering*.

These cracks in a rock demonstrate weathering

HOW DOES ICE CAUSE WEATHERING ?

Cracks in a road formed by frost heaves

Liquid water expands about nine percent when frozen. When water gets in the cracks of a rock, it can freeze and expand. This process is called *frost wedging*, which can lead to cracks getting bigger and parts of a rock breaking off. In the winter, roads often get bumps, or *frost heaves*, due to water freezing in the cracks and expanding.

HOW DO WAVES CAUSE WEATHERING ?

Waves pound against rocks with tremendous pressure. This pounding wears rock away. This is similar to how rounded sea glass forms on beaches. The waves, shells, and sediment in the water cause sharp, broken glass to smooth down over time.

Waves pounding at rocks

Tree roots uplifting and breaking apart a sidewalk

HOW DO ROOTS CAUSE WEATHERING ?

Roots are very strong. As they grow and extend, they break apart rock. Sidewalks that have trees nearby often have cracks due to expanding roots.

HOW DOES GRAVITY RESPOND TO WEATHERING ?

When loosened rocks roll or fall, they hit the ground and other objects. This causes more pieces of rock to break off. A landslide demonstrates what the force of gravity looks like on a large scale.

A rockslide in California

HOW DO ANIMALS CAUSE WEATHERING ?

Burrowing animals dig at the ground. Sharp claws can wear at rock causing it to crack and break apart. Groundhogs, foxes, and prairie dogs are examples of animals that use their claws to burrow into the ground. Other creatures, such as beetles and worms, also burrow into the ground making holes or tunnels. Humans are another animal that causes physical weathering through various methods like bulldozing, mining, and farming.

A prairie dog in the entrance to an underground burrow

HOW DOES THIS RELATE TO CAKE ?

Picture a cake left outside. The sun would dry it out, making it a bit like a rock. Animals would nibble at it and the rain would cause it to wear down. Another way this relates to cake is when you use a fork to eat it. You pick at the cake piece by piece, bite by bite, and in the process, various sizes of cake break off.

A fork breaking apart a piece of cake

WHAT IS EROSION ?

Coastal erosion in East Riding of Yorkshire, Great Britain

Erosion is the process by which rock or sediment moves from one location to another. Weathering will often lead to erosion by breaking off small pieces of rock or sediment, which can then be moved easily by wind, rain, waves, or the force of gravity. Some areas of land are more prone to erosion, such as beaches because of the wind and waves.

WHAT IS SEDIMENT ?

S ediment is a small piece of rock.

A variety of sediment sizes, ranging from very fine sand to pebbles

HOW DO YOU CLASSIFY SEDIMENT ?

S cientists classify sediment to help in their communication about rocks. The *Wentworth scale* classifies rock particles based on their size. A few categories of classification are boulder, pebble, very fine sand, coarse silt, and clay. To classify rock particles, *geologists* measure their grain size. For example, a pebble is 0.4cm to 6.4 cm across, while a piece of clay is less than 0.004mm across. Another way to classify sediment is by using the *Krumbein scale*, which measures the roundness of rock particles.

HOW DOES THIS RELATE TO CAKE ?

Much the way rocks have different sizes of sediment that break off, cakes have different sizes of crumbs. A cheesecake, for example, has tiny crumbs, more like clay, while pieces of coffee cake are much larger, like pebbles.

Cheesecake

WHAT IS DEPOSITION ?

After erosion, *deposition* occurs when rock or sediment settles. This process is called deposition because the sediment deposits in a location. Often this happens in calm water, where the sediment will start to build up and compress. Over time, this can lead to the formation of sedimentary rocks.

CONGLOMERATE CANDY CAKE

1 cup of various gummy candies (such as gummy bears)

2 cups of flour   1 cup of sugar

½ teaspoon of baking powder   1 pinch of salt

½ stick of butter (at room temperature)   ½ teaspoon of vanilla

2 eggs

1. Preheat oven to 350 degrees Fahrenheit.

2. Apply cooking spray to the base and sides of a loaf pan. Dust with flour.

3. Mix candies together. *The candy represents clasts (such as pebbles and gravel), which are part of a conglomerate rock.* Add two tablespoons of flour and stir well enough to coat the candies.

4. In a separate bowl, use an electric beater to mix the butter until creamy. Slowly add the sugar and continue to mix. Add the eggs one at a time. Mix in the vanilla, a pinch of salt, and the baking powder. Then, slowly add the flour while you continue to mix. *This batter represents the sediment that serves as a cement that holds the clasts in a conglomerate rock together.*

5. The batter should be dense. Using clean hands mix in the clasts (candy).

6. Press the batter into the pan. If possible, try to avoid having clasts (candy) touch the edge of the pan because they will melt. *A conglomerate rock has the pebbles and gravel intact, not melted.*

7. Bake about an hour. To make sure the cake is done, stick a toothpick in the center of the cake and remove it; the toothpick should come out dry. Let cake cool.

8. Carefully take a butter knife and run it along the inside edge of the cake pan, this will help loosen the cake from the pan. It may help to flip the pan upside down to release the cake.

9. *While cutting, think about the Mohs scale of mineral hardness. If there were a similar scale for cutting cakes, think about where this cake would fall on the scale.*

10. *While eating, pay attention to the clasts and how this cake represents a conglomerate rock. A conglomerate rock is composed of clasts, which are held together by a mixture of sediment, such as sand and clay.*

FOSSILS

WHAT ARE FOSSILS ?

Fossils are preserved remains or imprints of *organisms*.

Fossil of Priscacara clivosa, which lived approximately 50,000,000 (50 million) years ago

WHERE ARE FOSSILS FOUND ?

They are typically found in sedimentary rocks. Often an organism dies or the print of an organism is left in mud, silt, or sand. Over time, sedimentary rock can harden with the remains or prints intact.

An imprint of a shell fossilized into sedimentary rock

HOW DOES THIS RELATE TO CAKE ?

The candles on a cake are like organisms. The candles that have tipped over represent organisms that have died. They have compressed into the frosting, much like how the remains of an organism can compress into a sedimentary rock when it is forming. The candles that are lifted off of the frosting have left an imprint.

Candles and frosting demonstrating the phases of fossil formation

WHAT ARE TRACE FOSSILS ?

A *trace fossil* is evidence of a species from when it was alive, such as footprints. Trace fossils help scientists better understand information about species, such as the running speed of an animal or if they travelled in packs.

A dingo paw print

WHAT ARE CASTS AND MOLDS ?

A *mold* is formed when an organism makes an imprint on sediment, but leaves no physical remains. Over time, the sediment hardens with the imprint intact. For example, molds can be imprints of sea creatures in which the body washes away, but the print stays in place. A cast occurs when a mold is filled with sediment that compacts and eventually becomes a sedimentary rock. The cast creates a mirror-image replica of the imprint.

A cast of an ammonite, which lived approximately 150,000,000 (150 million) years ago

HOW DOES THIS RELATE TO CAKE ?

A cake pan represents a mold. The cake batter that is poured in the pan represents sediment that has deposited over time. When the cake bakes, it comes out in the exact shape of the pan; this represents a *cast fossil*.

The cake forms a replica of the cake pan

SEDIMENTARY CAST AND MOLD FOSSIL CAKE

2 sticks of butter (at room temperature)

1 cup of flour

1 cup of superfine or powdered sugar

1 teaspoon baking powder

2 tablespoons unsweetened cocoa powder

4 eggs

4 tablespoons of milk

1 teaspoon vanilla extract

1 pinch of salt

1. Preheat oven to 375 degrees Fahrenheit. *Please note that heat is <u>not</u> a part of sedimentary rock formation, but the oven is allowing us to fast forward through the time that it takes for sediment to deposit, compact, and cement into a sedimentary rock (this can potentially take millions of years).*

2. Mix butter and sugar with an electric blender. Add vanilla, then one egg at a time and continue to mix. Slowly add flour and continue to mix. Add the milk and blend until smooth. *This batter represents sediment.*

3. Put one third of the batter into a separate container and mix in the cocoa powder.

4. *The cake pan represents a mold, which is an imprint of an organism.* Apply cooking spray to the mold and dust with flour. Slowly pour the batter without chocolate into the pan. *This batter represents sediment depositing into a mold and building up over time. The chocolate batter represents another type of sediment.* Slowly swirl the chocolate batter into the mold.

5. Bake about 40 minutes. To make sure the cake it done, stick a toothpick in the center of the cake and remove it; the toothpick should come out dry. Remove cake and let cool.

6. Carefully take a butter knife and run it along the inside edge of the cake pan. This will help loosen the cake from the pan.

7. *Flip the mold upside down, releasing the cast.*

8. *While eating, pay attention to the shape of the cast and how it is an exact replica of the mold.*

EARTH'S HISTORY

HOW OLD IS EARTH ?

Geologists believe that Earth is over 4,500,000,000 (four and a half billion) years old.

Earth as seen from space

HOW DO GEOLOGISTS KNOW HOW OLD EARTH IS ?

The oldest rocks that geologists have dated on Earth are around 4,400,000,000 (four billion, four hundred million) years old. But geologists have dated rocks from the moon that are even older than this. The dates of these rocks and information from meteorites have led geologists to come up with their determination of how old Earth is.

WHAT DOES THE MOON'S AGE HAVE TO DO WITH EARTH'S AGE ?

Many geologists believe that the moon was once a part of Earth. Part of the basis for this theory is that rocks from the moon are similar to rocks from Earth. Many geologists believe that Earth was hit, in its early stages of formation, by a very large space rock. This collision caused part of Earth to break off. The piece that broke off became the moon. This theory is called the "giant impact hypothesis."

An artist's depiction of the "giant impact hypothesis"

HOW DOES THIS RELATE TO CAKE ?

Batter is an early stage of the process of a cake forming. The photographs represent this by showing how some of the batter was taken out of the bowl and baked separately from the rest of the cake. However, unlike the cupcake and large cake, which look the same, Earth and the moon have very different topography and climates.

Cake batter represents Earth and the moon having the same origin

A cupcake represents the Moon and the cake represents Earth

WHAT ARE THE LAYERS OF EARTH ?

The innermost layer of Earth is called the *inner core*, which is solid rock. The *outer core*, which follows, is liquid rock. Next is the *mantle*, which is 3,000 kilometers (around 2,000 miles) deep and is made primarily of solid rock. The mantle can be divided into the lower mantle and an upper mantle. The upper mantle contains softened rock, which Earth's *crust* floats on. The *lithosphere* is the term for the top of Earth's mantle and the crust. The crust includes the tectonic plates and the *biosphere*.

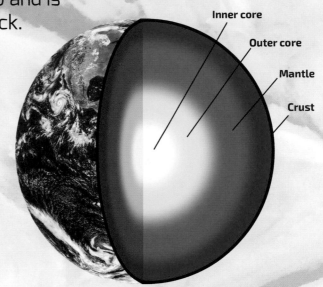

Inner core

Outer core

Mantle

Crust

Earth's Layers

WHERE DO WE LIVE ON EARTH ?

We live on the biosphere, which is part of Earth's crust. The biosphere has soil, trees, water, and all of Earth's organisms.

Salmon River, Idaho

HOW DOES THIS RELATE TO CAKE ?

In this picture, Earth's crust is like the frosting that surrounds the cake. Imagine all of the white frosting is completely covered by sprinkles; that would be Earth's biosphere. Just like Earth, the outside of the cake looks very different from the inner layers.

A cake with sprinkles representing Earth's biosphere

WHAT IS THE LAW OF SUPERPOSITION ?

The *law of superposition* is a method of dating rock layers based on how they build up over time. The deeper you dig into the ground, the older the rocks are. As a result, the surface of Earth, where we live, has the newest rocks. The layers of rock in canyons demonstrate the law of superposition and provide important evidence about Earth's past. For example, the oldest layer of rock in the Grand Canyon is at the bottom of the canyon and it is 1,840,000,000 (one billion, eight hundred forty million) years old.

View from the South Rim of the Grand Canyon

HOW DOES THIS RELATE TO CAKE ?

When this cake was made, the layer on the bottom was put down first. The layers then built up from there one by one, much like layers of rock build up. The icing represents the surface of Earth. The deeper down you go, the older the layers are.

To make this cake, you start with the bottom layer and build up

LAW OF SUPERPOSITION LAYER CAKE

〰️◇〰️◇〰️◇〰️◇〰️◇〰️◇〰️◇〰️◇〰️◇〰️◇〰️

2 cups of sugar

1 ¾ cups of flour

¾ cup of unsweetened cocoa powder

1 ½ teaspoons of baking powder

1 ½ teaspoons of baking soda

1 container of frosting

1 cup of boiling water (have adult supervision for this)

2 eggs

1 pinch of salt

1 cup of milk

½ cup of vegetable oil

2 teaspoons of vanilla extract

(If you double these ingredients, you can make a four-layer cake)

1. Preheat oven to 350 degrees Fahrenheit.

2. Apply cooking spray to the base and sides of two 9-inch round pans. Dust with flour.

3. Use an electric beater to mix flour, sugar, cocoa, baking powder, baking soda, and salt. Slowly add eggs, milk, oil, and vanilla and continue to mix until creamy. Carefully, stir in the boiling water. The boiling water will make the batter much less dense.

4. Pour batter into the pans and bake 30-35 minutes. To make sure the cakes are done, stick a toothpick in the center of one cake and remove it; the toothpick should come out dry.

5. Carefully take a butter knife and run it along the inside edge of the cake pans to help loosen the cakes. It may help to flip the pan upside down to release the cake.

6. Let cakes cool completely on a wire rack.

7. Put one cake down on a plate. *This cake represents the oldest layer of rock.* Put frosting on the cake, then add the next layer of cake. *This represents a newer layer of rock.* If you double the ingredients, you can make a cake that is four layers high. *The youngest layer is the one on top.*

8. *While cutting the cake, notice that your knife cuts through the newest layers of rock first, then works its way down to the oldest layer of rock.*

WHAT ARE TECTONIC PLATES ?

They are giant slabs of rock that float on softened rock. The continents and the ocean basin are a part of the plates. Tectonic plates can be up to 100 kilometers (60 miles) deep.

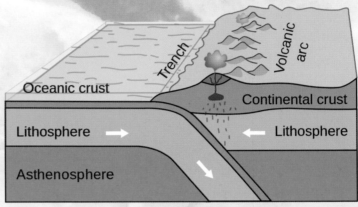

A visual representation of the tectonic plates

WHERE ARE THE TECTONIC PLATES ?

They are in the lithosphere, which includes the top portion of Earth's mantle and all of Earth's crust.

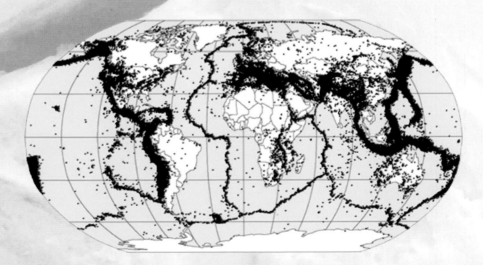

On this map, each black dot represents earthquake locations around the world. These dots create a visual outline of Earth's major tectonic plates.

DO TECTONIC PLATES MOVE ?

The tectonic plates move a few inches every year. Over millions of years, this adds up to a big change in the position of the continents on Earth. The plates are able to move because they float on slightly softened rock in the upper layer of Earth's mantle, called the **asthenosphere**.

HOW DOES THIS RELATE TO CAKE ?

Much as the top layer of this cake sits on top of the icing, tectonic plates sit on top of the softer asthenosphere. You can shift the top and bottom layer of this cake because of the soft icing.

The top piece of cake
can move on the icing

HOW DO TECTONIC PLATES FIT TOGETHER ?

They fit together by touching side by side. Tectonic plates can move toward each other, meeting at a **convergent** plate boundary. This pressure can lead to mountains forming. Tectonic plates can also move away from each other, leaving a **divergent** plate boundary. Into the small gap left behind, magma instantly rises and hardens into new rock. When plates slide along each other, they create a **transform** plate boundary, where sudden jerks in the sliding movement can lead to earthquakes.

WHAT IS PANGAEA ?

Alfred Wegener came up with the theory of *continental drift*. He found evidence that the continents were once joined together and are slowly moving apart. Wegener named this supercontinent of the past *Pangaea* (meaning "all lands"). Geologists have determined that Pangaea existed around 300,000,000 (300 million) years ago.

The continents separating from the supercontinent, Pangaea, to where they are today

HOW DOES THIS RELATE TO CAKE ?

Wegener was looking at a map of Earth and noticed how the continents look as if they could fit together. This is much as if you looked at pieces of cake and realized that they were once a part of a whole cake.

Cake pieces in various directions represents the continents today

The cake pieces were once part of a whole cake

TECTONIC PLATE CAKE

1 stick of butter (at room temperature)

1 cup of sugar

1 egg

1 teaspoon of vanilla extract

2 cups of flour

½ cup of unsweetened cocoa powder

1 ½ teaspoons of baking soda

½ teaspoon of baking powder

1 pinch of salt

1 cup of milk

1 container of whipped frosting

1. Preheat oven to 350 degrees Fahrenheit.

2. Use an electric beater to mix the butter, sugar, eggs, and vanilla until creamy. Slowly add milk and continue to mix.

3. In a separate bowl, mix flour, cocoa, salt, baking soda, and baking powder.

4. Slowly add the flour mixture and stir until it is an even consistency.

5. Drop spoonfuls of mixture onto an ungreased cookie sheet.

6. Bake for 8-12 minutes. The larger the spoonfuls, the longer the cooking time. To make sure the cakes are done, stick a toothpick in the center of one cake and remove it; the toothpick should come out dry. Remove cakes and let cool. *The cakes represent Earth's tectonic plates.*

7. After the crust has cooled, put frosting between two pieces of crust. *The frosting represents the upper portion of Earth's mantle (the asthenosphere). The tectonic plates float on the asthenosphere.*

8. *Before eating, slide the tectonic plates (cake) over the asthenosphere (frosting). The cake moving and sliding serves as a model of tectonic plate movement.*

EARTH IN SPACE

WHY DOES EARTH EXPERIENCE DAY AND NIGHT ?

It takes 24 hours for Earth to make one rotation. This is why there are 24 hours in a day. When we are facing the sun, it's daytime. When we are facing <u>away from</u> the sun, it is nighttime. At any given moment, it is daytime for half of the planet and nighttime for the other half.

WHY DO WE HAVE SEASONS ?

Earth is angled at a 23.5-degree tilt, which causes the sun's rays to hit Earth with different amounts of light. At any given moment, one hemisphere of Earth is tilted <u>toward</u> the sun and the other hemisphere is tilted away from the sun. When a hemisphere is tilted <u>toward</u> the sun, it's summer. When a hemisphere is tilted <u>away from</u> the sun, it's winter. This is why the seasons are opposite in the northern and southern hemispheres. In the image above, it is summer in the southern hemisphere and winter in the northern hemisphere. The direct or indirect angle of the sun also explains why there are more hours of sunlight in the summer and fewer in the winter. The equator, however, has the same angle of sunlight hitting it year round so it does not experience seasons.

HOW DOES THIS RELATE TO CAKE ?

A cake pop is held up straight, but Earth is not. It's at a 23.5-degree angle.

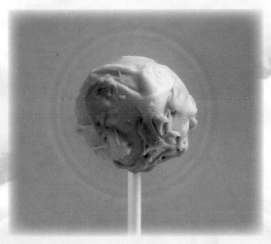

An upright cake pop

A cake pop at an angle

The cake pop stand below shows Earth's orbit around the sun. The toothpick represents the axis from North Pole to South Pole, allowing you to see how Earth is tilted. This tilt causes seasons because hemispheres experience either direct or indirect sunlight, which affects the sun's intensity and the number of hours of sunlight and darkness that are experienced each day.

A cake pop stand demonstrating the seasons

HOW BIG IS OUR GALAXY ?

Our galaxy, the Milky Way, is so big that even if you traveled at light speed, you couldn't journey across it in your lifetime. It would take about 100,000 years to make the journey. Our galaxy is just one of billions in the universe.

A galaxy similar to our Milky Way galaxy

HOW DOES THIS RELATE TO CAKE ?

Picture Earth as one grain of sugar. Now imagine the Milky Way as a cake with all of its ingredients (stars, planets, black holes, etc.). If Earth is represented by one grain of sugar, then the Milky Way would be a cake that is around 40,000,000 (40 million) kilometers or 25,000,000 (25 million) miles wide. That's a REALLY big cake!

One 0.5mm grain of sugar represents Earth

EARTH CAKE POP

1 ½ cups of flour

1 cup of sugar

1 ¾ teaspoons of baking powder

1 stick of butter (at room temperature)

2 eggs

12 cake pop sticks

2 teaspoons of vanilla extract

½ cup of milk

1 container of frosting

1 package of blue candy melts

1 package of green candy melts

1. Preheat oven to 350 degrees Fahrenheit.

2. Mix butter and sugar until creamy. Add eggs and stir, then add vanilla, flour, and baking powder and stir. Slowly add milk and stir until evenly mixed.

3. Pour batter into a 9x13" baking pan and bake around 25 minutes. To make sure the cake is done, stick a toothpick in the center of the cake and remove it; the toothpick should come out dry.

4. Let the cake cool, then crumble up the cake in a bowl. Add three heaping spoonfuls of store bought frosting. Use your clean hands to mix together; giving the mix an even consistency. The crumbs should stick together (add more frosting if necessary). Put in refrigerator for one hour.

5. Round cake pops with your hand. They should be about the size of a ping-pong ball. Refrigerate for 20 minutes.

6. Melt blue candy melt in accordance with the package's directions. Add a teaspoon of vegetable oil and stir (be sure that no water is added to the candy melt). Dip end of cake pop stick into the candy melt and stick into the cake pop. Do not put the stick in too far or the cake will crumble and fall apart. Put sticks in all of the cake pops.

7. Dip each cake pop in blue candy melt (you may need to spoon candy melt over the cake pops). *This represents Earth's oceans.* Allow cake pops to fully cool.

8. Melt green candy melt in accordance with the package's directions. Dip a toothpick into the green candy melt and paint on the shape of the continents. Let cake pops cool.

9. *Before eating, tilt the cake pop at a 23.5-degree angle to simulate Earth's tilt.*

glossary

asthenosphere	upper portion of Earth's mantle that the tectonic plates float on
biosphere	the outer part of Earth's crust; where life is
cast fossil	a replica of a mold, but not the actual organism
clast	broken off fragments of rock
conglomerate	a sedimentary rock made of clasts that are cemented together
continental drift	the theory that the continents are moving
convergent	a boundary where tectonic plates move towards each other
crust	the most exterior layer of Earth
deposition	the process of rocks or sediment settling in a location
divergent	a boundary where tectonic plates move away from each other
erosion	the process of rocks or sediment moving
extrusive	igneous rocks that form on the surface of Earth
foliated	a rock with layers
fossils	remains or imprints in rocks caused by an organism
frost heaves	bumps in the road caused by frost wedging
frost wedging	when rocks break because of water freezing and expanding
geologist	someone who studies geology
geology	the study of Earth and what it is made of
igneous rock	rock made from hardened magma or lava
inner core	the innermost core of Earth
intrusive	igneous rocks that form inside the ground

Krumbein scale	a scale of rock particle roundness
lava	what magma is called after it erupts from a volcano
Law of superposition	the deeper you go into the ground, the older the rocks are
lithosphere	the top portion of the mantle and Earth's crust
magma	melted rock, also called molten rock
mantle	Earth's layer between the outer core and crust
metamorphic rock	rock that changed forms due to heat and/or pressure
mineral	a hard substance that can form rocks
Mohs scale	a scale that measures mineral hardness
mold	a print of an organism, but not the actual organism
non-foliated	a rock without layers
organism	anything living or once living, such as a plant or animal
outer core	a liquid rock layer after Earth's inner core
Pangaea	Alfred Wegener's term for Earth's super continent
physical weathering	(or *mechanical weathering*) movements that cause rock to break down
rock cycle	a continuous cycle in which rocks change form
sediment	small broken down pieces of rock (sand, pebbles, etc.)
sedimentary rock	rock made of sediments compacted and cemented together
trace fossil	evidence of an organism, such as footprints, but not remains
transform	a boundary where tectonic plates slide past each other
weathering	the process of rocks or sediment breaking down
Wentworth scale	a scale of rock particle size

about the author

Katie Coppens lives in Maine with her husband and two children. She is an award-winning middle school language arts and science teacher. Katie has multiple publications, including a teacher's guide for the National Science Teachers Association entitled *Creative Writing in Science: Activities That Inspire*. For more information on her publications, please visit *www.katiecoppens.com*.

acknowledgments

I would like to thank the amazing staff at Tumblehome Learning! Barnas Monteith's excitement for this manuscript and love of geology made all of this possible. Penny Noyce's integration of science and literacy is an inspiration and her editing feedback made the book what it is today. Yu-Yi Ling deserves thanks for somehow saving the cake in the author's photo from the unexpected wave that hit us during the photo shoot and the amazing job she did with the book's layout.

Thank you to my past and present students who inspired the idea for this book by showing me how effective cake could be as a teaching tool. It all started with carrot cake to demonstrate the difference between minerals and rocks and then it kept going from there!

Thank you to my geology professor Dr. Nels Forsman, who provided feedback on the manuscript, confirmed the scientific accuracy of the concepts, and came up with the granite rock recipe. I am grateful for his additions to the book and for all that he has taught me about geology.

Thank you to my friend, and astrophysicist, Dr. Grant Tremblay. Grant completed the mathematical conversions to determine the scale of the Milky Way if Earth was the size of a grain of sugar (0.5mm).

Thank you to my sister for her encouragement. Thank you to my dad for helping edit some of the cake photographs and for his years of "tech support." Thank you to my mom who loved to find interesting rocks and listen to me talk about them.

Thank you to my husband for his endless support (with everything from posing as a hand model to helping me with rounds and rounds of cake-related dishes). And thank you to my daughters for all the smiles we had while eating lots and lots of cake!

sources

Forsman, Nels. Personal communication, December 2016.

"Giant Impact Hypothesis." *Wikipedia.* Wikimedia Foundation. Web. 24 Nov. 2014. http://en.wikipedia.org/wiki/Giant_impact_hypothesis

"Grain Size." *Wikipedia.* Wikimedia Foundation, 24 Nov. 2014. Web. 25 Nov. 2014. http://en.wikipedia.org/wiki/Grain_size

"How Many Galaxies Are There?" *Space.com.* Web. 24 Nov. 2014. http://www.space.com/25303-how-many-galaxies-are-in-the-universe.html

"How the Moon Formed: Lunar Rocks Support Giant Impact Theory." *Space.com.* Web. 24 Nov. 2014. http://www.space.com/26142-moon-formation-giant-impact-theory-support.html

Maton, Anthea. *Dynamic Earth.* Englewood Cliffs, NJ: Prentice Hall, 1997. Print.

"Mohs Hardness Scale." *Testing the Resistance to Being Scratched.* Web. 12 Aug. 2016.

"Perisphinctes." *Wikipedia.* Wikimedia Foundation. Web. 29 Aug, 2016.

"Priscacara." *Wikipedia.* Wikimedia Foundation. Web. 29 Aug, 2016.

Tarbuck, Edward J., Frederick K. Lutgens, and Dennis Tasa. *Earth: An Introduction to Physical Geology.* Boston, MA: Prentice Hall, 2011. Print.

"The Planetary Society." *The Planetary Society Blog.* Web. 24 Nov. 2014. http://www.planetary.org/multimedia/space-images/charts/wentworth-1922-grain-size.html

"Theories of Formation for the Moon." *Theories of Formation for the Moon.* Web. 24 Nov. 2014. http://csep10.phys.utk.edu/astr161/lect/moon/moon_formation.html

Tremblay, Grant. Personal communication, August 2016.

photo credits